A Donation has been made to the
Clay County Public Library In
Memory Of:

Jack Jones

This Donation has been made by:

Geraldine Clark

MOTORMANiA

SPORTS CARS

Written by
PENNY WORMS

A+
Smart Apple Media

Published by Smart Apple Media,
an imprint of Black Rabbit Books
P.O. Box 3263, Mankato, Minnesota 56002
www.smartapplemedia.com

Cataloging-in-Publication Data is available from
the Library of Congress
ISBN: 978-1-59920-993-7   (library binding)
ISBN: 978-1-68071-012-0   (eBook)

The author would like to thank Felix Wills and
the following for their kind help and permission
to use images: Jeremy Davey from the Thrust
team; Dave Rowley from the Bloodhound team;
and the media teams at Audi, BMW and McLaren.

Picture Credits
007 Magazine Archive/EON Productions: 24b. Ben
Pipe Sports/Alamy: 20. Eric Charbonneau/WireImage for
Disney Pictures: 21b. Getty Images: 16b. Graham
Harrison/Alamy: 21cr. GUMPERT Sportwagenmanufaktur
GmbH, www.gumpert.de: 7cr, 18/19 (Uli Jooss), 19cr.
KOENIGSEGG Automotive AB: contents page, 26/27.
Pagani Automobili S.p.A.: 12/13 (all images). René Staud
Studios: 24/25. Shutterstock: 6/7, 16t, 17 & cover.
Transtock Inc/Alamy: 10 bottom. BUGATTI Automobiles
S.A.S., www.bugatti.com: 8/9. www.carphotolibrary.
co.uk: title page, 7t, 9t, 9b, 10t, 14, 15t, 15b, 22t, 22b, 23,
24t. McLaren, www.mclaren.com: 11.

Printed in the United States by Jaffe Book Solutions,
St. Louis, Missouri

Disclaimer: Some of the "Stats and Facts" are
approximations. Others are correct at time of writing,
but will probably change.

3-2017

CONTENTS

SPORTS CARS	6
BUGATTI VEYRON	8
McLAREN F1 LM	10
PAGANI ZONDA F	12
FERRARI F430 SCUDERIA	14
DODGE VIPER SRT10	16
GUMPERT APOLLO	18
PORSCHE 911 GT3	20
CHEVROLET CORVETTE Z06	22
ASTON MARTIN DBS	24
KOENIGSEGG CCX	26
GLOSSARY	28
INDEX	30

SPORTS CARS

For many people, sports cars are the most exciting and desirable cars on the road. From the popular Mazda Miata to the various supercars in this book, all these vehicles are designed and built for speed, and to offer a thrilling driving experience.

RACING

Many sports car makers, such as Ferrari and Porsche, have become well known through their success on the race track. They use what they learn from their racing cars to improve the design and performance of their road cars.

JAGUAR E-TYPE

When Jaguar introduced the E-Type in 1961, it rocked the sports car world. They had combined good looks and high performance at an affordable price. It started a golden time in sports car history. The E-Type is still considered one of the best sports cars of all time.

BUILDING THE BEST

When creating a sports car, there are six important things to consider: speed, power, design, safety, luxury, and road **handling**. Handling means how quickly and smoothly the car responds when steering or changing gears.

Gumpert Apollo design sketches

BUGATTI VEYRON

The Bugatti Veyron is one of the fastest **production cars** in the world, with a top speed of 407 km/h (253 mph). Going at this speed, it can drive from one end of a football field to another in one second. It is also one of the heaviest, most comfortable, and luxurious of the supercars.

THE KEY TO SPEED

To reach top speed, the driver must stop the car and turn the "top-speed key." The car drops down to 2.5 inches (6.5 cm) from the ground, the rear **spoiler** goes up, and the front **air vents** shut. The car is ready. At full **throttle**, it burns the entire 26-gallon (100-l) fuel tank in just 12 minutes.

Rear spoiler

Front air vents

STATS AND FACTS

- **Top speed:** 253 mph (407 km/h)
- **0-60 mph:** 2.5 seconds
- **Country of origin:** Italy
- **Cost:** $1.5 million
- **Claim to fame:** The ultimate luxury supercar with staggering speed and amazing **technology**.

RAW POWER

The Veyron has a super-powerful 1,000-bhp V12 engine. The term **bhp** stands for **brake horsepower**, which means this engine has the pulling power of 1,000 horses. The V12 means that the engine has 12 cylinders. Inside these cylinders, little explosions take place when gasoline is burned. This generates the power to move the car.

GRAND SPORT

The open-top Veyron Grand Sport was revealed in 2008. Bugatti designed it to be just as fast, safe, and comfortable, but it does come at a higher price.

McLAREN F1 LM

The McLaren F1 LM is one of the world's rarest sports cars. It is a special edition McLaren F1 and only five have been produced—one for every F1 that finished an astonishing Le Mans race in 1995. Le Mans is the most famous car race in the world and the F1s came first, third, fourth, fifth, and thirteenth. LM stands for Le Mans.

THE McLAREN F1

In the 1990s, McLaren unveiled the F1. It was the fastest production car ever and it held that record for seven years. It recorded a top speed of 241 mph (391 km/h), even faster than the F1 LM.

NO FRILLS

In both the F1 and the F1 LM, the driver sits in the middle like a race-car driver. There are no luxuries like comfy seats or a car stereo. There would be no point in having a stereo. The engine noise is loud—even when the car is standing still!

- **Top speed:** 225 mph (362.1 km/h)
- **0-60 mph:** 2.9 seconds
- **Country of origin:** Great Britain
- **Cost:** $1.2 million
- **Claim to fame:** Only five F1 LMs exist—each one is now priceless.

PAPAYA ORANGE

All LMs are painted "papaya orange." This is because Bruce McLaren, the man for whom the McLaren car company is named, used this color on cars he used to race. Team McLaren is still a successful Formula One team.

PAGANI ZONDA F

The Pagani Zonda F is a hand-built, high-performance Italian sports car. Pagani makes only about 15 cars a year, and every detail is beautifully designed and crafted. The body is made from **carbon fiber**, not metal, because carbon fiber is lightweight and rigid.

POWERFUL ENGINE

The engine is made by Mercedes-Benz and is one of the biggest 12-cylinder engines ever produced. Because the car is so light, the engine can produce instant **acceleration** that thrusts you back into your seat.

- **Top speed:** 214 mph (345 km/h)
- **0-60 mph:** 3.5 seconds
- **Country of origin:** Italy
- **Cost:** $1.3 million
- **Claim to fame:** Each Zonda F is unique. Every owner gets a special owner's manual with his or her new car.

AERODYNAMIC

The design of the Zonda is incredibly **aerodynamic**. It can easily cut through the air at high speed. Air flows over the top, but also through the vent at the front. This creates **downforce** (*see page 18*), meaning that the **air pressure** helps to push the car down on to the road or track.

POWERFUL BRAKES

The braking power of the Zonda is as impressive as its acceleration. At 125 mph (200 km/h), it takes only 4.4 seconds to come to a complete stop. This is roughly the same time as an average car traveling at half the speed.

FERRARI F430 SCUDERIA

This is a high-performance Ferrari with Formula One technology. The F430 Scuderia is a special edition based on the Ferrari F430, built for the real driving **enthusiast**. It is a thrill to drive, and with just a flick of a switch, it is ready for the race track.

Air vents

DISTINCTIVE DESIGN

Like the F430, the Scuderia has two large air vents at the front. These suck in air as the car drives along to cool down the engine parts. Where it differs is that it often has two stripes down the top, from front to back.

STATS AND FACTS

- **Top speed:** 198 mph (318.7 km/h)
- **0-60 mph:** 3.1 seconds
- **Country of origin:** Italy
- **Cost:** from $260,000
- **Claim to fame:** Formula One legend Michael Schumacher helped Ferrari to develop the car.

FINGER-TIP CONTROLS

The Scuderia steering wheel is more like the steering wheel of a Formula One car than a sports car. It is actually a computer. A switch called the "Mannetino" changes the way the car drives.

SPORT is for normal driving.
LOW-ROAD HANDLING is for wet and slippery roads.
RACE switches off most of the safety features built into the car, making it ready for racing.

LOSING WEIGHT

The F430 Scuderia is all about performance. To make it faster, Ferrari made it lighter—it is 221 pounds (100 kg) lighter than the standard F430. This means that the engine doesn't need so much power to shift the Scuderia from a standing start. It also looks more like a racing car inside, with all unnecessary things like carpets stripped away.

DODGE VIPER SRT10

The Dodge Viper is an American-built sports car with a 20-year history. From the start, it was designed and built to be all brute force and power, with none of the high-tech gadgets or fine handling of its European competitors. That achieved, the Viper is not only fast, it's fun.

MONSTER ENGINE

The most **exceptional** thing about the Viper is the engine. Originally from a truck, it was turned into a V10 monster with the help of Italian sports car experts Lamborghini. The sound isn't like a roar. It's more of a growl from an angry grizzly bear rushing out of its cave to eat whomever has woken it up!

TORQUE

There are two measures of how powerful a car is: bhp and **torque**. To put it simply, horsepower is what moves the car along. Torque is the force that pulls the car from a standstill or up a hill. The Viper engine has 600 horsepower and 560 **lbs ft** of torque. These numbers add up to awesome acceleration.

STATS AND FACTS

- **Top speed:** 190 mph (305.8 km/h)
- **0-60 mph:** 3.9 seconds
- **Country of origin:** USA
- **Cost:** $85,000
- **Claim to fame:** It had its own TV show in America called "Viper."

RED DEVIL

Originally, all Vipers used to be red, but the SRT10 can be ordered in a range of colors. The stripes cost extra, but their impact is priceless.

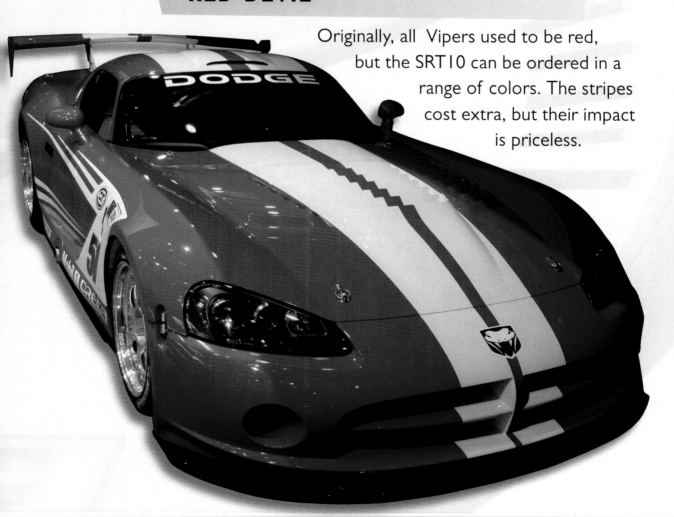

GUMPERT APOLLO

The Gumpert Apollo is a remarkable car. It is claimed that it could drive upside down along the ceiling of a tunnel without falling off. The science behind the claim is mind-boggling, but it is all to do with downforce. Has it been done? No one has been crazy enough to try it!

LOW-FLYING VEHICLE

Gumpert calls the interior the "cockpit" and the driver "the pilot." Their aim is to come as close to the feeling of flying as you can get while driving a car.

DOWNFORCE

Creating downforce is like controlling air and gravity. It's very important to sports car designers because it is the thing that keeps a car glued to the track or road when traveling at high speed. Without downforce, a car might lose control—or, worse still, take off!

- **Top speed:** 224 mph (360 km/h)
- **0-60 mph:** 3 seconds
- **Country of origin:** Germany
- **Cost:** $410,000
- **Claim to fame:** Was once the fastest car around the race track on the TV program "Top Gear."

ALL ABOARD

Getting into the Apollo is not what you would expect. The doors lift up like a bird's wings. You have to take off the steering wheel to get in and the seats don't adjust. But this car is not built for comfort. It is built for speed.

PORSCHE 911 GT3

The Porsche 911 was launched 40 years ago, and its distinctive design has changed little over that time. It is still one of the most desirable sports cars around. But the launch of the 911 GT3 shows that Porsche hasn't been sitting back enjoying their success. The technology and **engineering** are right up there with the best.

READY TO RACE

Customers wanting to race their Porsche GT3 can order the sports package at no extra cost. This includes a bolted-on **roll cage** behind special bucket seats, and a racing harness instead of seat belts. There is even an built-in fire extinguisher.

STATS AND FACTS

- **Top speed:** 194 mph (312 km/h)
- **0-60 mph:** 4.1 seconds
- **Country of origin:** Germany
- **Cost:** $124,000
- **Claim to fame:** An absolute sports car classic with a long racing history.

TRUNK POWER

Like most Porsches, the engine is in the back. The GT3 engine produces more power than any other 911 but has similar **fuel consumption**— it can go 13 miles on a gallon of gas (that's 5.5 kilometers to the liter).

FILM STAR

Someone at the film company Pixar obviously thinks the Porsche 911 is a beautiful car. They chose one to be Lightning McQueen's love interest, Sally, in the film *Cars* (2006).

CHEVROLET CORVETTE Z06

The Corvette is probably the most famous American sports car. Produced by General Motors since 1953, the Corvette was the first ever American two-seater sports car. General Motors has continued to develop this **iconic** car, and the Z06 is one of the fastest of them all.

STING RAY

Since 1953, there have been seven generations of Corvette, from the C1 to today's C7. The Z06 is a version of the C6. The famous Sting Ray was a version of the C2 in the 1960s. The Sting Ray is the ultimate classic American sports car.

A CHEVY WITH ATTITUDE

The Z06 looks almost the same as other Corvettes. The only sign that it is a much more powerful model is the four exhaust pipes at the back. Chevrolet claims that it is ready for the track as soon as it leaves the showroom, but whether you buy it for racing or for the road, you get a lot of car for a relatively low price.

STATS AND FACTS

- **Top speed:** 198 mph (318.7 km/h)
- **0-60 mph:** 3.6 seconds
- **Country of origin:** USA
- **Cost:** $90,000
- **Claim to fame:** Rock star Prince wrote a song about one: "Little Red Corvette."

MATERIAL MIX

The secret to the Z06's speed is that it is super light. It is made from lightweight **aluminium**, carbon fiber and, **titanium**. The floor is made of balsa wood. The paint on the wings weighs more than the wings themselves!

Front wings

ASTON MARTIN DBS

Aston Martin is a British sports car company with a long and successful racing history. Now they are most admired for producing beautiful, comfortable sports cars. The DBS is the latest model, with every detail refined.

LUXURY

The interior of the DBS is roomy, with hand-finished leather trim and comfy bucket seats. There's no key to start the car. Instead there is a high-tech "Emotional Control Unit" made of sapphire. Slide it in, push it, and the car roars to life.

BOND'S CAR

Aston Martins are famous for being driven by the fictional British spy James Bond 007. Daniel Craig, who played Bond in both in *Casino Royale* (2006) and *Quantum of Solace* (2008) drove a grey DBS. In *Casino Royale,* a DBS was rolled a record-breaking seven times in a single stunt.

STATS AND FACTS

- **Top speed:** 191 mph (307 km/h)
- **0-60 mph:** 4.3 seconds
- **Country of origin:** Great Britain
- **Cost:** $250,000
- **Claim to fame:** James Bond's latest Aston Martin. He's also had a DB5, Vantage, and Vanquish.

GRAND TOURER

Jeremy Clarkson, on the TV car program *Top Gear*, summed up what makes the DBS special. He said he would happily drive it to the south of France (13 hours from London), and if he found he'd left his swimming trucks at home, he'd happily drive it back again!

KOENIGSEGG CCX

Koenigsegg is a small Swedish company that has made a big mark on the sports car world in recent years. The CCX is a luxury supercar with a **futuristic** design, luxury interior, and high-performance engine.

GOING UP

The Koenigsegg CCX looks quite different from other sports cars. It looks like a car Batman would drive. The hard top comes off and can be stored under the hood, and the doors swivel up, not out.

The engine is in the back.

STATS AND FACTS

- **Top speed:** 245 mph (395 km/h)
- **0-60 mph:** 3.2 seconds
- **Country of origin:** Sweden
- **Cost:** $1 million
- **Claim to fame:** The CCX held the world record for the fastest production car (broken by the Ultimate Aero).

CUSTOMER SATISFACTION

Every CCX is created specifically for each customer. A small team of 17 at the Koenigsegg workshop build the cars. Customers can choose everything from the color to whether they want fitted luggage and cupholders. The interior is beautifully designed and standard features include a built-in phone and navigation system.

GOING GREEN

Koenigsegg has also produced the CCXR, the first "green" supercar. It can run on **biofuel** as well as gasoline. Biofuel is made from organic matter, such as plants and cow manure. It is an "eco" alternative to gas and diesel.

GLOSSARY

acceleration an increase in speed

aerodynamic designed to travel through the air quickly and easily

air pressure when air pushes down toward earth

air vents holes in the body of a car that allow air in to cool parts that get hot

aluminium a lightweight metal that resists rust

biofuel a type of fuel, often made from plants

brake horsepower (bhp) a way of measuring how powerful an engine is when a type of brake is applied

carbon fiber a material made of little strings of carbon, a substance even stronger than metal. The fibers are lightweight and flexible

downforce the force caused by air rushing over a moving car that forces it down on to a track or road

engineering the use of science in designing and building

enthusiast somebody who is very interested in something

exceptional extra special

fuel consumption how much fuel a car uses, usually measured by how far a car can go on one gallon

handling how a car feels to drive; how it responds

iconic something that, over time, has become an icon or symbol

lbs ft the way torque is measured, shortened from "pounds feet"

production cars cars that are made in a factory and sold to anyone

roll cage a strong metal frame built into a car that protects the driver if the car crashes or rolls over

spoiler a car part that makes a car more aerodynamic because it "spoils" the way air drags a car and slows it down. A spoiler forces air up and improves downforce.

technology the use of science and the latest equipment

throttle the pedal on a car that you press to go faster (it releases fuel into the engine)

titanium a strong metal that resists rust

torque the force that makes a car move from a standstill or power up a hill

INDEX

A

aerodynamics 13, 28, 29
Aston Martin DBS 24-25

B

Bond, James 24, 25
braking power 13
Bugatti Veyron 8-9

C

Chevrolet Corvette Z06 22-23
Clarkson, Jeremy 25
Craig, Daniel 24

D

Dodge Viper SRT 10 16-17
downforce 13, 18, 19, 28

F

Ferrari 6, 14-15
Ferrari F430 Scuderia 14-15
Formula One 11, 14, 15

G

General Motors 22
Gumpert Apollo 7, 18-19

J

Jaguar E-Type 7

K

Koenigsegg CCX 26-27

L

Le Mans 10

M

Mazda MX-5 6
McLaren F1 LM 10-11

P

Pagani Zonda F 12-13
Porsche 6, 20-21
Porsche 911 GT3 20-21
production cars 8, 10, 29

S

Schumacher, Michael 15
Sting Ray 22

T

"Top Gear" 19, 25
torque 16, 29